Read Write Inc. SPELLING

Series developed by Ruth Miskin

Contents

Introduction	2
Read Write Inc. Spelling resources	2
Get Spelling! Books	4
Spelling Log Book	10
Assessment	10
Classroom management	12
Scope and sequence of *Read Write Inc. Spelling*	16
The English alphabetic code	19
Get Spelling! Book 1 Introductory activities	19
Get Spelling! Introductory activities lesson plans	21
Get Spelling! Key activities example lesson plans	26
Appendices	32
Appendix 1: *Get Spelling! Book 1* Photocopiable Introductory Activities	32
Appendix 2: Red word activities	36
Appendix 3: Roots and suffixes	38
Appendix 4: Extra dictation sentences	39
Appendix 5: Answers	45
Appendix 6: Word banks	50
Appendix 7: *Read Write Inc. Spelling* and the Primary Framework for Literacy	56

Introduction

We love spelling

Some children learn to spell effortlessly – most get there in the end, but too many find the process of learning to spell arduous, painstaking and, sadly, boring.

Spelling must be made fun, enjoyable and interesting. The Friday spelling test may be great for those who can already spell, but for others it makes for a scary Friday morning: most children get most spellings right on the day, but forget them hours later; others just get them wrong.

We only get really good at spelling by practising over and over again. And if we are going to practise something a lot, it is better that we enjoy doing it.

Who will benefit from *Read Write Inc. Spelling*?

This spelling programme is for children who have completed *Read Write Inc. Phonics* or who are already *reading* at National Curriculum level 2a or above, or English Language Guidelines 5–14 Level B and above.

The spelling programme should ideally be used alongside *Read Write Inc. Comprehension* which groups children by their reading ability. However, it can be used successfully with schools not using *Read Write Inc. Phonics* or *Comprehension* as it assumes that children have basic phonic knowledge from other programmes.

Read Write Inc. Spelling resources

Three *Get Spelling! Books* for learning, practising and assessing spelling

A *Spelling Log Book* for logging words to practise, spelling tips, and an ongoing assessment tool

Read Write Inc. Spelling Handbook

Read Write Inc. Spelling resources

Get Spelling! Books

Children should complete all the activities in the three *Get Spelling! Books* (see page 26). There are introductory activities in *Get Spelling! Book 1* which explain the whole alphabetic system to the children*. Those children who can spell reasonably well can then move quickly through the units in *Get Spelling! Book 1*.

For children who have completed *Read Write Inc. Phonics*, *Get Spelling! Book 1* provides a thorough revision of *Speed Sounds* Lessons 2 and 3 as well as more work on roots and suffixes. The words children spell in *Get Spelling! Books 2* and *3* build upon what they have learnt in *Book 1*.

There are eight spelling activities in each unit in the *Get Spelling! Books*. Activities 1, 2, and 3 require teaching, and Activities 4, 5, 6, 7 and 8 children complete with their partners and then mark with you. These activities focus on graphemes, roots, prefixes and suffixes.

The same types of activities are used in all three books. This means that as the children progress through the programme you will spend less time explaining the activities and more time teaching children how to spell. *Example lesson plans for the activities in the Get Spelling! Books are provided on pages 26–31 of this Handbook.*

There are also 'red words' (common words with an irregular spelling) to learn in each unit. Notes on using mnemonics and other strategies for remembering red words are given in *Information check* in the *Example lesson plans* on page 26. In *Get Spelling! Books 2* and *3* you select which of the red words the children need to practise each week.

Homophones (words which sound the same but are spelt differently, e.g. 'wait' and 'weight') are also taught.

The programme is based on over learning; the English alphabetic system is the most complex in the world and needs a lot of practice to achieve proficiency in spelling. As children work all the way through the three books, they keep a log of the words they have found the most challenging, while you keep a log of common words that the children spell incorrectly in their own writing. These words are constantly revised all the way through the programme though the *Spelling Log Book* reviews, the Two minute check and the Spelling challenge.

---

* *These are reproduced on pages 32–35 of this Handbook for any children not starting on Get Spelling! Book 1.*

Read Write Inc. Spelling resources

Get Spelling! Book 1

1. Information check
Children practise spelling 88 red words (common words with unusual spelling) using techniques such as mnemonics, raps, words-in-words and 'naughty' letters.

Homophones
Homophones are introduced in every unit.

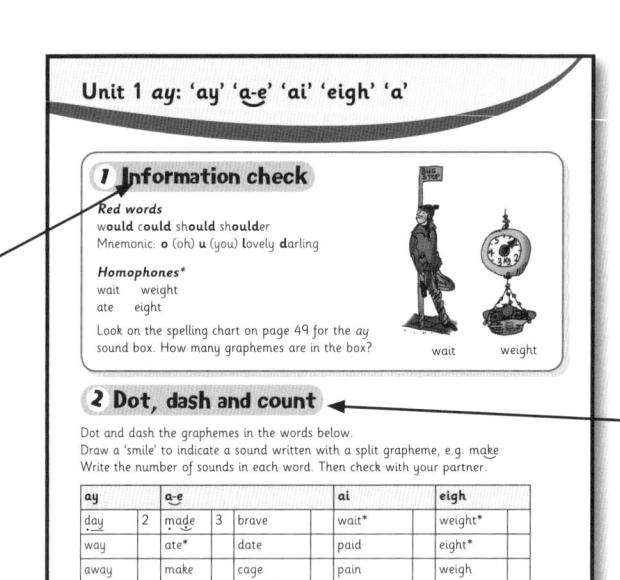

2. Dot dash and count
Children are taught the alternative spelling for the same sound in single and multi-syllable words.

Unit 1 *ay*: 'ay' 'a-e' 'ai' 'eigh' 'a'

1 Information check

Red words
would could should shoulder
Mnemonic: **o** (oh) **u** (you) **l**ovely **d**arling

*Homophones**
wait   weight
ate   eight

Look on the spelling chart on page 49 for the *ay* sound box. How many graphemes are in the box?

2 Dot, dash and count

Dot and dash the graphemes in the words below.
Draw a 'smile' to indicate a sound written with a split grapheme, e.g. make
Write the number of sounds in each word. Then check with your partner.

ay		a-e		ai		eigh	
day	2	made	3	brave		wait*		weight*	
way		ate*		date		paid		eight*	
away		make		cage		pain		weigh	
stray		take		escape		train		**a**	
delay		came		mistake		fail		apron	
today		gave		chocolate		afraid		table	
Monday		save				complain		able	
holiday						explain			
birthday									

Tips: ★ 'ay' always comes at the end of a root word.
★ 'a-e' is the most common spelling of this vowel sound.

6

Read Write Inc. Spelling resources

3. Write the root
Children are taught the impact of suffixes on key root words.

3 Write the root

Write the root word.

Tip: Remember that when the suffix 'ing' is added to a root word, the final 'e' is dropped. Say: 'You can't have an E with an I-N-G.'

suffix -s	root
days	
pays	
delays	

suffix -ing	root
making	
taking	
escaping	
mistaking	

suffix -ed	root
strayed	
delayed	
waited	
contained	
complained	
escaped	

suffix -er	root
braver	
straighter	

suffix -est	root
bravest	
straightest	

4 Word fill

Choose the correct word to write in each space. Then check it with your partner.

wait   weight   way   weigh   eight   ate

1. What is the _____ of the cake? It looks very heavy.
2. How long will I have to _____ for the bus?
3. I have eaten too much cake. How much do you think I _____?
4. I do not know which _____ to go.
5. Kate is _____ years old.
6. Who _____ all the chocolate cake?

7

4. Word fill
Children practise spelling the homophones in the context of sentences.

5. Circle the right one
Children select the correct spelling from other incorrect spellings of the same word, and begin to assess their knowledge of words learnt so far.

5 Circle the right one

Circle the correct spelling.

1 escapt   escaped
2 holidays   holydays   hollidays
3 making   makeing   macking
4 straigt   strat   straight
5 bravest   bravist
6 choclate   choclut   chocolate

Check with your partner.
Then check your answers in your dictionary.

6 Four-in-a-row game

Take turns to spell a word from the lists in Activities 2 and 3. (Don't look!)
Write the words in a jotter.
Tick a circle if it's correct. If not, correct the bit that's wrong.
The winner is the first to spell four words in a row correctly.

○○○○   ○○○○   ○○○○   ○○○○

6. Four-in-a-row game
Partners take turns in assessing each other's knowledge of the week's words.

7 Dictation

Take turns to read aloud the dictation sentences from Unit 1, pages 45 and 47, for your partner to write in a jotter – no peeping!
Correct any errors your partner may have made. Swap after each sentence.

7. Dictation
Partners assess each other's spelling knowledge using dictation sentences.

8 Spelling Log

Choose five words from Activities 2 and 3 that you find most challenging. Write them in the grid on page 8 of your Spelling Log Book. Circle the part of the word that you found most difficult to remember and explain why to your partner. Discuss with your partner how you will remember how to spell the word.

8

8. Spelling Log
Children identify the words they would like to review in subsequent weeks.

5

Read Write Inc. Spelling resources

Get Spelling! Book 2

1. Information check
Children explore different spellings of the same consonant sound.

Red words
Children continue to practise spelling the 88 red words (common words with unusual spelling) using techniques such as mnemonics, raps, words-in-words and 'naughty' letters.

Unit 6: '-al' '-il' '-el'

1 Information check

Red words
Write down your red words to learn:

_____

-al -il -el
When we say the words in the chart in Activity 2 below, the last syllable sounds like *le* as in 'little'.
Read the words in the chart in 'full value' syllables by pronouncing:

★ 'medal', 'usual' to rhyme with 'pal' – e.g. *med-al*
★ 'pupil', 'pencil', 'April' to rhyme with 'fill' – e.g. *pu-pil*
★ 'parcel', 'jewel' to rhyme with 'bell' – e.g. *par-cel*

This will help you spell them correctly.

2 Dot, dash and count

Dot and dash the graphemes in the words.
Write the number of sounds in each syllable.
Then check with your partner.

pu-pil	2 + 3	grad-u-al	
A-pril		i-den-ti-cal	
pen-cil		roy-al	
an-gel		e-qual	1 + 3
jew-el		in-di-vi-du-al	
med-al		med-ic-al	
us-u-al		trad-i-tion-al	

17

---

2. Dot, dash and count
Children apply their knowledge of sound-grapheme correspondences from *Get Spelling! Book 1* with alternative consonant spellings to spell words syllable-by-syllable.

Read Write Inc. Spelling resources

3. Write the root
Children apply their wide knowledge of prefixes and suffixes to the root words above.
They learn that from one root word many others can be made.

3 Write the root
The '-ly' suffix has been added to the words below. Now write the root.

root	suffix -ly
	usually
	individually
	medically
	traditionally
	equally
	gradually

4 Word fill
Choose the correct word to write in each space. Then check with your partner.
gradual   gradually   usual   usually   equally   equal

1. The water was so cold that people could only get in _____.
2. The slope was very _____ so I could cycle easily.
3. I _____ have sandwiches for my lunch.
4. We will walk to school today, as _____ _____.
5. Please divide the cake _____ between your friends.
6. That is not fair. You have not made the pieces _____.

4. Word fill
Children practise writing the root word with prefixes and suffixes in the context of a sentence.

5 Circle the right one
Circle the correct spelling.

1. usually   usualy
2. pencle   pencil   pencul
3. usual   usuall
4. identical   identicul
5. gradually   gradully

Check with your partner. Then check your answers in your dictionary.

18

5. Circle the right one
Children select the correct spelling from other incorrect spellings of the same word, and begin to assess their knowledge of words learnt so far.

6. Four-in-a-row
Partners take turns in assessing each other's knowledge of the week's words.

6 Four-in-a-row game
Take turns to spell a word from the lists in Activities 2 and 3. (Don't look!)
Write the words in a jotter.
Tick a triangle if it's correct. If not, correct the bit that's wrong.
Now choose a word for your partner to write.
The winner is the first to spell four words in a row correctly.

△△△△   △△△△   △△△△   △△△△

7 Dictation
Take turns to read aloud the dictation sentences from Unit 6, pages 44 and 46, for your partner to write in a jotter – no peeping!
Correct any errors your partner may have made. Swap after each sentence.

7. Dictation
Partners assess each other's spelling knowledge using dictation sentences containing the week's words.

8 Spelling Log
Choose five words from Activities 2 and 3 that you find the most challenging. Write them in the grid in your Spelling Log Book page 25.
Circle the part of the word you find most difficult to remember and explain to your partner why. Discuss how you will remember how to spell the word.

8. Spelling Log
Children identify the words they would like to review in subsequent weeks.

19

Read Write Inc. Spelling resources

Get Spelling! Book 3

1. Information check
Children are taught word origins of key words to show them how words have been constructed from other languages.

Red words
Children continue to practise spelling the 88 red words (common words with unusual spelling) using techniques such as mnemonics, raps, words-in-words and 'naughty' letters.

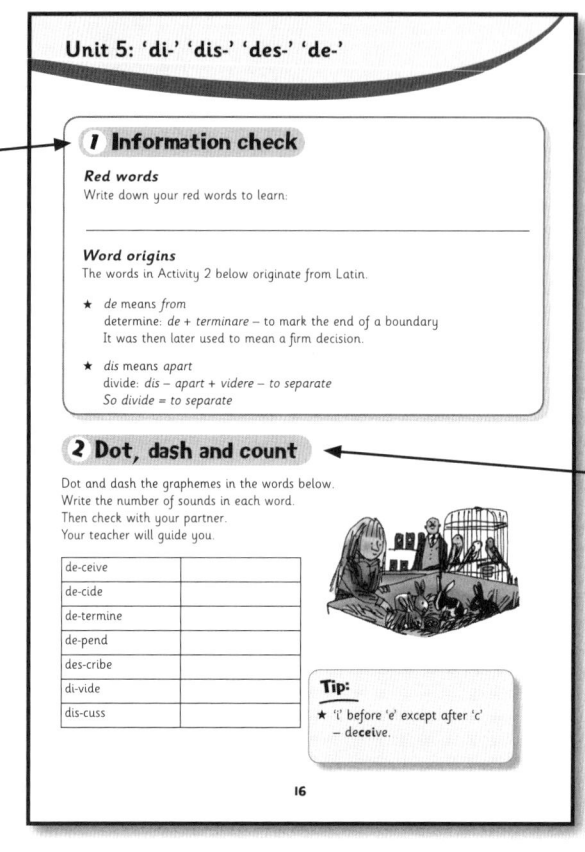

2. Dot, dash and count
Children use their knowledge of sound-grapheme correspondence to spell words syllable-by-syllable.

3. Write the root
Children apply their wide knowledge of prefixes and suffixes to the root words above.
They learn that from one root word, many others can be made.

Unit 5: 'di-' 'dis-' 'des-' 'de-'

1 Information check

Red words
Write down your red words to learn:

Word origins
The words in Activity 2 below originate from Latin.

★ *de* means *from*
   determine: *de* + *terminare* – to mark the end of a boundary
   It was then later used to mean a firm decision.

★ *dis* means *apart*
   divide: *dis* – *apart* + *videre* – *to separate*
   So divide = to separate

2 Dot, dash and count

Dot and dash the graphemes in the words below.
Write the number of sounds in each word.
Then check with your partner.
Your teacher will guide you.

de-ceive	
de-cide	
de-termine	
de-pend	
des-cribe	
di-vide	
dis-cuss	

Tip:
★ 'i' before 'e' except after 'c' – dece**i**ve.

3 Write the root

Write the root, prefix and suffix. Your teacher will guide you.
deceive: to pretend to be or do something, mislead
You deceived me by telling me you were ill when, actually, you went shopping.

root	+ suffix	root + suffix
deceive	-ing	
	-ed	
	-tion	deception
	-tive	

Tip: You can't have an E with an ING, e.g. deceive deceiving.

decide: to make up your mind about something
I cannot decide whether I want the yellow or the green T-shirt.

root	+ prefix or suffix	root + prefix or suffix
decide	-ing	
	-ed	
	-sion	
	-ive	decisive
	in- + -ive	

determined: to decide definitely to do something.
I am determined to save up enough money to buy a laptop.

root	+ prefix or suffix	root + prefix or suffix
determine	-ed	
	-ation	
	un- + -ed	

describe: explain, tell
Describe your new house to me.

root	+ prefix or suffix	root + prefix or suffix
describe	-ed	
	-ing	
	-tion	description
	-ive	
	in- + -able	

Read Write Inc. Spelling resources

4. Word fill
Children practise writing the root word with prefixes and suffixes and choose one of the words to write in a sentence of their own.

---

discuss: talk about, argue, chat about
Let's discuss your problem and try to find an answer.

root	+ suffix	root + suffix
discuss	-ed	
	-ing	
	-ion	

divide: split, separate, break up, share out
Divide the cake so we all get the same size piece.

root	+ suffix	root + suffix
divide	-ed	
	-ing	
	-sion	

4 Word fill

Decide the correct word to write in the spaces. Then choose one of the words to write in a sentence of your own in a jotter.

1. **decide decision indecision decisive indecisive**
   Helen is always sure of what she wants to do; she is very _____.

2. **determination determined undetermined**
   You need lots of _____ if you want to climb to the top of Mount Everest.

3. **discussion discussed discussing**
   We sat up all night _____ what was the best way to solve our problem. Having a _____ is so important before reaching an agreement.

18

---

5. Circle the right one
Children select the correct spelling from other incorrect spellings of the same word, and begin to assess their knowledge of words learnt so far.

6. Four-in-a-row
Partners take turns in assessing each other's knowledge of the week's words.

5 Circle the right one

Cover up Activity 4 Word fill.
Circle the correct spelling and change the incorrect spellings.

1 desicion decision dicision   3 division divishon divission
2 decieve deceive   4 discussion discusion disscussion

Check with your partner.
Then check your answers in your dictionary.

6 Four-in-a-row game

Take turns to spell a word from the lists in Activity 3. (Don't look!)
Write the words in a jotter.
Tick a star if it's correct. If not, correct the bit that's wrong.
Now choose a word for your partner to write.
The winner is the first to spell four words in a row correctly.

☆☆☆☆ ☆☆☆☆ ☆☆☆☆ ☆☆☆☆

7 Dictation

Take turns to read aloud the dictation sentences from Unit 5, pages 47 and 48, for your partner to write in a jotter – no peeping!
Correct any errors your partner may have made. Swap after each sentence.

8 Spelling Log

Choose five words from Activity 3 that you find most challenging. Write them in the grid on page 38 of your Spelling Log Book.
Circle the part of the word that you found most difficult to remember and explain why to your partner. Discuss with your partner how you will remember how to spell the word.

19

7. Dictation
Partners assess each other's spelling knowledge using dictation sentences containing the week's words.

8. Spelling Log
Children identify the words they would like to review in subsequent weeks.

9

Read Write Inc. Spelling resources

Spelling Log Book (see page 30)

Children keep a personal *Spelling Log* of words they find hard to remember.

After each unit in the *Get Spelling! Books* children decide the five words they find most difficult to spell from that unit and 'log' them in the grapheme chart for that unit in their *Spelling Log Book*.

They also choose two 'red words' to practise. The *Spelling Log Book* can be taken home.

Book 1 Unit 6 ou: 'ou' 'ow'

Write in your words to learn for the week.
Write the tricky part of the word in big letters to help you remember it.

ou
shout

ow
cow

★ Red words to learn

★ Words to review

13

Children may practise spelling the words at home. They can review three old words and practise seven new words each week; every time the child spells the word correctly the parent writes the date and their initials next to the word in the Log.

Assessment

Assessment is integral to the programme. Each unit of work starts with teaching activities and follows with partner and individual assessment and practice activities.

As the programme progresses, children learn that there are essentially three groups of words:

1. Words they *know* they can spell.
2. Words they can often spell, but sometimes misspell when engrossed in writing: these are words that children continue to practise. Underline these words for children to correct. These words are collected in their *Spelling Log Book*.
3. Unusual and adventurous words they have a go at spelling phonetically 'legally' while writing, which will be corrected, lightly, by you when marking. Children do not look in the dictionary while writing as this stops the flow of thoughts and ideas.

Read Write Inc. Spelling resources

Spelling challenge

At the end of each term organise a Spelling Challenge by collecting 50–100 words from the children's *Spelling Log Books* and your own log. (These will vary according to the group.)
Children who have been working at the same level are put into groups of four. The aim is to see how many words each group can score together. The groups practise these spellings with their group during the Spelling Challenge week. Children may also take the list home.

Show the children how to work together to maximise the potential of the group.
1. Children go through their list individually and tick the words they really *know* they know.
2. The group then makes one joint list of the words that are not ticked.
3. Children take it in turns to be the caller. The caller identifies 5–10 words from the list. The group decide the difficult part in each word and the caller circles this.
4. The caller:
   - Calls out one of these words
   - Asks the other children in the group to write the word in a jotter
   - Corrects any part of the word that is wrong
   - Calls out the other 5–10 words until the group know them.

Children take turns being the caller each day until the group can spell as many words as possible. On the Spelling Challenge day, call the words for each group. (If there is more than one level of spelling, call out the words in turn.) The joint scores of all the children in each group are totalled. The winning group nominates a treat that is of benefit to all the groups.

Classroom management

How much time is needed?

The programme aims to get children to National Curriculum Level 5 (English Language 5–14 Level D/E). If children practise the activities for at least ten minutes a day from Year 2 (Primary 3), once they can read at National Curriculum Level 2a and above (English Language 5–14 Level B), allowing extra time on the first few units for you and the children to get used to the programme, most children will only need light touch revision in Years 5 and 6 (Primary 6 and 7). The children's level of achievement is assessed by their application of the spelling knowledge taught in these books. Those who are fortunate in having a good visual memory will soon be spelling at a Level 4+ level (English Language 5–14 Level D+). Others will need a lot more revision and practice during the junior years. See the suggested schedule on page 27.

By the end of the spelling programme, the children with quick memories will only need a to practise the more complex words added to their *Spelling Log Books*. The other children continue to practise the words collected in their *Spelling Log Books* by using Activity 6: *Four-in-a-row*, Activity 8: *Spelling Log* and by you doing a *Two minute check*.

How should the children be grouped?

Try to group children according to their spelling progress. Children need to be reading at National Curriculum Level 2a (or at English Language 5–14 Level B and above) before they start this programme, so in a Year 3 (Primary 4) class, some may still be following *Read Write Inc. Phonics* as they are reading below National Curriculum Level 2a (English Language 5–14 Level B), some may be working at a steady pace through *Read Write Inc. Spelling*, while others will be whizzing through it. The closer the homogeneity of the group, the more confident the children will be and the faster they will progress.

Here are three possible groupings.
1. Set across one or more year groups for the literacy hour. Although the groups will be determined by reading ability, all the children can work together, day-by-day.
2. Set across a year group for spelling for just ten to fifteen minutes a day.
3. Teach your own class group and split the children who are reading at Level 2a (English Language 5–14 Level B) and above into two or three groups according to broad spelling ability. Alternate the groups that you teach and those who complete the practice and assessment activities. If children are below this level they should follow *Read Write Inc. Phonics*.

How important is partner work?

Children should work with a partner who is at about the same level of spelling ability; they can have more fun learning and can help each other as well. When children discuss the words they are learning to spell, it is more likely they will remember them.
If you are teaching an individual child, you may choose to be the second partner. (However don't do this if you are teaching a group.)

Classroom management

Deciding partnerships

In all circumstances, the teacher decides on the partnerships. Partnerships should be chosen with care and rotated every few weeks.

It is important to consider how well different children will work together. If there is a child who is particularly difficult, choose his/her partner carefully. Explain, privately, to the partner why he has been chosen, how much you appreciate his patience, and how hard you see him working. Be wary of over-using the same child to deal with more challenging children.

Try to avoid odd numbers, but if this is unavoidable, put three well motivated children together.

Possible partnerships

- Pair a lively child with an assertive, well-behaved child.
- Pair two dominating children. (They can take turns to listen.)
- Pair two shy children. (Someone has to talk!)
- Mix boys and girls, levels of maturity, first and second language learners as much as possible.

Remember, if a question is worth asking, it's worth everyone answering. All children should answer all questions by discussing them with their partners. (The only exception to this is when a group is given specific questions. In these circumstances, the whole group should answer.) Whatever the question, children should never raise their hands. If this is allowed, you will give the message that only a few need to answer.

In order to establish good partner work, it is important to examine, with the children, what is involved in working with a partner.

Where do children sit during the lesson?

Children sit at their tables, side-by-side with a partner, with easy view of you, the board, the Spelling chart, a 'Red word wall' and a 'Vocabulary wall'.

Red word wall

Display all the 'red words' at the start of the programme. Teach these words throughout other lessons as well as in the spelling lesson (see Key spelling activities notes). Touch or point to the words as you do this.

Vocabulary wall

If you are using *Read Write Inc. Phonics* and *Read Write Inc. Comprehension*, you will already have a pocket chart or wall devoted to exciting new vocabulary from the stories the children read. Add any new words from the *Get Spelling! Books* that will expand children's vocabulary – make sure they know their meanings!

Classroom management

Positive Teaching

Children learn at a much faster pace in an assertive and positive climate. They talk more readily in an atmosphere free of anger and tension. Shouting, nagging and 'shushing' have a derimental effect on children's talking and therefore on their learning.

Catch them being good! Try to praise children whenever there is an opportunity. Praise them explicitly for specific things. Teachers know their childen; some children prefer quiet, private praise, while others are happy for it to be shared with the group. Praise them, in particular, for their partner work. As they overhear the explicit praise, others will copy the good partner behaviour.

Pace

A brisk pace is essential. Childen should be working so hard that they do not have any 'down time'. If the pace is too slow, children become restless and there is more potential for challenging behaviour to start.

Purpose

Every part of a lesson has a specific purpose. It is important to keep that purpose clear in your mind as you teach.

Passion

This is a very prescriptive programme, which is why it works so well. However, it is the energy, enthusiasm and passion that teachers put into the lessons that bring the teaching and learning to life. Pedestrian teaching will not have the same impact as passionate teaching!

Classroom management

Management signals

The 'stop' signal
When all the children are answering every question, you must be able to gain their attention quickly and easily, without the need to raise your voice.
Hold your hand up in the air. Do not talk while the hand is raised. The children then finish what they are saying, raise their hands in response, and check that others have seen the signal, gently tapping on arm if necessary (avoiding poking with elbows and saying 'oi'). Do not start talking until everyone has returned the signal. If the signal fails, lower your hand and remind the children of the school's expectations. Explain that all the adults in the school will be using the stop signal. The children must return the signal to any adult who uses it.

The 'my turn, your turn' signal
There are times in the programme when you will need the children to copy what you do.

My turn: touch your chest with your palm when it's your turn.
Your turn: open your palm to the children when it's their turn.

The 'turn to your partner' signal (TTYP)
Before you ask a question, tap two fingers together to warn the children that they will need to turn to their partners to answer.
Explain that the 'hands up' system for answering questions will not be used. (However, 'hands up' for clarification and for asking further questions should be encouraged.)

The 'perfect partner position' signal
When you say 'Get ready', the children should get into their 'perfect partner positions' for spelling. Partners should sit side-by-side and shoulder-to-shoulder. (If they face each other, the noise level increases.) Decide which children will be Partner 1 for this session. The other is Partner 2.

Scope and sequence of Read Write Inc. Spelling

Get Spelling! Book 1

	44 speech sounds (24 *consonant* speech sounds, 20 *vowel* speech sounds)
Unit 1	Words with **ay**: ay, a–e, ai, eigh, a, e.g. d**ay**, m**a**d**e**, w**ai**t, **a**pron, w**eigh**t + suffixes **s**, **ed**, **ing**, **er**, **est**
Unit 2	Words with **ee**: ee, ea, e, y e.g. s**ee**, t**ea**, w**e**, bod**y** + suffixes **s**, **es**, **ed**, **ing**, **er**
Unit 3	Words with **igh**: igh, i-e, ie, y, i, e.g. h**igh**, l**i**k**e**, l**ie**, f**i**nd, b**y** + suffixes **s**, **es**, **ed**, **ing**, **y**, **er**
Unit 4	Words with **ow**: ow, o-e, oa, o, e.g. kn**ow**, br**o**k**e**, b**oa**t, s**o** + suffixes **s**, **es**, **ed**, **ing**
Unit 5	Words with **oo**: oo, u-e, ew, ue, oe, e.g. t**oo**, fl**u**t**e**, bl**ew**, bl**ue**, sh**oe** + suffixes **s**, **ed**, **ing**, **er**, **est**
Unit 6	Words with **ou**: ou, ow, e.g. l**ou**d, c**ow** + suffixes **ed**, **ing**, **ly**, **er**, **est**
Unit 7	Words with **ar**: ar, a (southern accents only) e.g. c**ar**, f**a**st + suffixes **s**, **es**, **ed**, **ing**, **er**, **est**
Unit 8	Words with **ir**: ir, ur, er, e.g. g**ir**l, h**ur**t, h**er** + suffixes **s**, **es**, **ed**, **ing**, **y**, **er**, **est**
Unit 9	Words with **air**: air, are, ear, e.g. ch**air**, squ**are**, w**ear** + suffixes **ed**, **ing**, **y**, **er**, **est**
Unit 10	Words with **or**: or, oor, ore, aw, e.g. **or**, d**oor**, s**ore**, s**aw**, + suffixes **ed**, **ing**, **s**, **er**, **est**
Unit 11	Words with **oy**: oy, oi, e.g. b**oy**, b**oi**l + suffixes **ed**, **ing**, **es**, **y**, **er**, **est**
Unit 12	Words with **ear**: ear, eer, ere, e.g. h**ear**, ch**eer**, + suffixes **ed**, **ing**, **s** Words with **ire**: ire, e.g. f**ire** + suffixes **ed**, **ing**, **s**
	Contractions/'Squeezed' words

Scope and sequence of *Read Write Inc. Spelling*

Get Spelling! Book 2

Unit 1	Words with **soft c**, e.g. **c**ity, ra**c**e + suffixes **s**, **ing**
Unit 2	Words with **soft g**, e.g. **g**entle, bri**dge**, cabba**ge** + suffixes **s**, **es**, **ing**, **ed**, **ly**
Unit 3	**Unusual plurals**, e.g. kni**ves**, potato**es**, bab**ies**, sheep, women
Unit 4	Short vowel doubling + suffixes **ed**, **ing**, **er**
Unit 5	Words ending in **le**, e.g. cudd**le**, batt**le** + suffixes **ed**, **ing**, **er**, **s**
Unit 6	Words ending with **il**, **el**, **al**, e.g. pup**il**, parc**el**, med**al** + suffix **ly**
Unit 7	Words ending in **en**, **an**, **on**, **in** + suffixes, e.g. gard**en**, ir**on**, wom**an** + suffixes **s**, **es**, **ed**, **ing**, **er**, **ly**
Unit 8	Words ending with suffixes **tion**, **sion**, e.g. atten**tion**, televi**sion**
Unit 9	Words ending with **ent**, **ant** e.g. transpar**ent**, import**ant**
Unit 10	Words ending with **ence**, e.g. pati**ence**, and **ance**, e.g. extravag**ance**
Unit 11	Words ending with **ous**, **cious**, **tious**, e.g. fam**ous**, deli**cious**, cau**tious** + suffix **ly**
Unit 12	Words ending with **schwa**: **ure**, **or**, **our**, e.g. nat**ure**, act**or**, col**our** + suffixes **ed**, **ing**
Unit 13	Words ending with suffixes **ible** and **ibly**, **able** and **ably**, e.g. horr**ible**, horr**ibly**, comfort**able**, comfort**ably**
Unit 14	Words ending with suffixes **ful** and **fully**, e.g. cheer**ful**, thank**fully**

Scope and sequence of Read Write Inc. Spelling

Get Spelling! Book 3

Root words, below, with all suffixes and prefixes taught in *Book 1* and *Book 2*:

ed	tion	ly	able	ible	ant	ent	er	ment
ing	sion	ally	ably	ibly	ance	ence	or	

+Negative prefixes

un	in	dis	ir	il

Root words

Unit 1	accept, accident, accommodate, admire, address, adventure
Unit 2	affect, agree, appear, appreciate, appoint, attract
Unit 3	compare, compete, complain, complete, compute
Unit 4	concentrate, congratulate, conscience, conscious, continue
Unit 5	deceive, decide, determine, depend, describe, discuss, divide
Unit 6	educate, exaggerate, excel, except, excite, exhaust, explain
Unit 7	illustrate, imagine, important, intelligent
Unit 8	prepare, pretend, prevent, present, produce, provide
Unit 9	repeat, remove, refuse, relate, responsible
Unit 10	'ch' = k, sh, e.g. chemist, machine
Unit 11	'ph' = f, e.g. physical
Unit 12	'que' = k, '-gue' = g, e.g. antique, catalogue

Negative prefixes   **un**able, **un**suitable, **un**repeatable, **un**adventurous, etc
disagree, **dis**grace, **dis**continue, etc
indecisive, **in**describable, **in**tolerant, **in**accurate, etc
irregular, **ir**relevant, **ir**responsible

Derivative roots   aqua, aer, mini, super, tele, trans, bene, bi, di, tri

The English alphabetic code

English has, probably, the richest vocabulary in the world with so many words that have similar meanings. Over the last thousand years we have inherited thousands of words from other languages and made them our own by homogenising the pronunciation until adopted Latin, French, Greek and German words all sound like English. However, we have also kept the spellings of these words, which has created the most complex alphabetic language in the world.

German, Italian, Spanish, Finnish, Polish, Greek and Welsh children learn to read and spell quickly because their speech sounds are written down, more or less, the same way in every word — so once they have cracked the code they can write any word correctly. This means they have a simple alphabetic code.

English, however, has many ways of writing each sound because we have more speech sounds and have inherited so many spellings from different languages. This makes the code so much harder to learn. For example, we write the sound 'ay' at least eight ways: pl**ay**, r**ai**n, m**a**k**e**, **eigh**t, str**aigh**t, r**eig**n, r**ei**n, br**ea**k. This means the alphabetic code takes a long time to learn. Anyone writing an English spelling programme is actually trying to put order into a language where there is little order!

This programme has been based, in the main, on the understanding that we do have a sound based writing system, albeit a very complex one! A given person uses the same 44 sounds to speak all English words. (The 44 sounds vary a little, accent to accent.) We need to remember that our own 44 sounds are consistent even though the way we write down the sounds is inconsistent. So one of the keys to good spelling is to remember how to spell these sounds in different words — and this does not happen over night. Even now, as adults, we avoid using words we cannot spell.

Just as a quick test, which of these words are spelt incorrectly?
supacede   brocolli   aparent   consede   proceede   idiosincracy
concensus   accomodate   impressario   rhythym   optholmologist
diptheria   anomoly   caesaerean   grafitti   diaharrioah

Spelling improves all through our lives, so it is unrealistic to expect children to spell every word in English correctly by the end of this programme! It is only with lots of practice that we become 'good enough' spellers. By the way, none of the words above are spelt correctly.

The English alphabetic code: *Get Spelling! Book 1* introductory activities

Children need: *Read Write Inc. Get Spelling! Book 1* pages 2–5, a spelling jotter and a sharp pencil. You need: the spelling chart (see page 24) and a pen.

- Letters written without inverted commas and in italics indicate that you need to say the sound of the letter, e.g. f: *fff*.
- Inverted commas indicate that you need to say the spelling of the sound (grapheme) in letter names. e.g. 'f': *eff*.

The English alphabetic code

Before you start to teach this programme it is very important that you understand it thoroughly yourself. Please read the information below and complete the activities. The *Read Write Inc. Phonemes Pronunciation Guide DVD* explains how to pronounce the sounds as 'pure' sounds and will help you to practise them.

Introduce the English alphabetic code.

Tell the children that:
- We use 44 speech sounds to speak every word in the English language, e.g. d-o-g, c-l-a-p, s-t-a-n-d.
- Every word we speak is made up of individual speech sounds that are spoken so quickly that we hardly notice them.
- When you spell any word, you are writing down these speech sounds, e.g. 'dog': d-o-g (3), 'shop': sh-o-p (3), 'clap': c-l-a-p (4) and 'stand': s-t-a-n-d (5).

Show the spelling chart:
- Explain that there are 44 sound boxes – one sound in each box.
- Teach the children the sound in each box. (Use the 'My-turn-your-turn' signal.)
- Explain that each of the 44 speech sounds is spelled with one, two or three letters. Each spelling is called a grapheme. Grapheme means 'writing' in Greek, e.g.
  – the sound *ay* is spelled 'ay' in day, 'ai' in train, 'a-e' in make and 'eigh' in eight
  – the sound *f* is spelled 'f' in fun, 'ff' in huff and 'ph' in phone.
- There are always the same number of speech sounds and graphemes in a word even though there may be more letters, e.g.
  – cat has three speech sounds: *c-a-t* and three graphemes: 'c'-'a'-'t'
  – other examples are *sh-o-p* (3), *l-igh-t* (3) and *g-r-ee-n* (4).
- Tell the children that as we have only 26 letters to write all these 44 speech sounds, letters are used in different combinations to write different sounds.

Get Spelling! Introductory activities lesson plans

See pages 2–5 of *Get Spelling! Book 1.*

INTRODUCTORY ACTIVITY 1

Purpose: to teach children how to pronounce the 44 speech sounds

Tell the children that:
- There are 24 *consonant* speech sounds and 20 *vowel* speech sounds.
- Consonant sounds are split into stretched sounds and bounced sounds: the stretched speech sounds can be as long as you can hold your breath; the bounced speech sounds are short and cannot be stretched.

Stretched sounds

Show the children how to say the stretched speech sounds below after you (using the 'My turn, your turn' signal). Make sure they do not say 'uh' at the end of each sound (*lllll* not *luh*; *mmmmm* not *muh*; *nnnn* not *nuh*; *ffff* not *fuh*; *sssss* not *suh*; *shhhh* not *shuh*).

Ask the children to take turns with a partner to listen to each other say the sounds.

f	l	m	n	r	s	v	z	sh	th	*th*	ng / nk

Bounced sounds

Show the children how to say the bounced speech sounds: *b* not *buh*; *c* not *cuh*.
(The two boxes with ! in, are really two speech sounds said at the same time. Please say them quickly and count them as one.)

Ask the children, with their partners, to take turns in listening to each other say the sounds.

b	c	d	g	j	p	qu !	t	w	x !	y	ch

The vowel speech sounds

Show the children how to say the vowel speech sounds below after you (using the 'My-turn-your-turn' signal), and then to practise with their partners.

a apple	e egg	i insect	o orange	u umbrella	ay play	ee see	igh high	ow snow	oo zoo
oo book	ar car	or for	air fair	ir girl	ou shout	oy boy	ire fire	ear hear	ure pure

Get Spelling! Introductory activities lesson plans

INTRODUCTORY ACTIVITY 2

Purpose: to teach children that one sound is often spelt in more than one way

Ask the children to look at the charts in the activity. Remind them that there is one speech sound in each sound box. Point out that each word in the lists has one grapheme written in bold, e.g. '**ph**oto'.

To demonstrate the grapheme in each word, use the 'My-turn-your-turn' signal to:
- point to and read '**ph**oto'
- say the grapheme '**ph**' (letter names)
- say the *f* speech sound and write '**ph**' in the box.

Repeat with each word.

photo hu**ff** be**ll** la**mb** autu**mn** **kn**ow **gn**aw fu**nn**y **wr**ap ca**rr**y **c**ircus pa**ss** pie**ce** gi**ve** bu**zz** wa**s** cau**ti**on spe**ci**al

f	l	m	n	r	s	v	z	sh	th *as in thumb*	th *as in this*	ng
ph	ll	mn	nn	wr	c	ve	zz	ti			
ff	le	mb	kn	rr	ss		s	ci			
			gn		ce						

ru**bb**le, du**ck**, **ch**emist, da**dd**y, gi**gg**le, **g**erm, ju**dge**, bar**ge**, ha**pp**y, bo**tt**le, **wh**ich, ca**tch**

b	c	d	g	j	p	qu	t	w	x	y	ch
bb	ck	dd	gg	g	pp	!	tt	wh	!		tch
	ch			dge							
				ge							

h**ea**d, g**y**m, m**a**k**e**, tr**ai**n, dr**ea**m, happ**y**, k**i**t**e**, t**ie**, b**y**, sm**o**k**e**, t**oe**, g**o**, bl**ue**, ch**ew**, p**u**t, f**a**ther, sn**ore**, p**oor**, l**aw**, **au**thor, b**ur**n, h**er** br**ow**n sp**oi**l d**eer** h**ear** c**are** advent**ure**

a	e	i	o	u	ay	ee	igh	ow	oo
ea	y				a–e	ea	i–e	o–e	ue
					ai	y	ie	oe	ew
							y	o	
oo	ar	or	air	ir	ou	oy	ire	ear	ure
u	a	ore	are	ur	ow	oi		eer	
		oor		er					
		aw							
		au							

Get Spelling! Introductory activities lesson plans

INTRODUCTORY ACTIVITY 3

Purpose: for children to count the number of speech sounds in each word, including multi-syllabic words

Show the children how to:
- say each word in this activity in speech sounds
- draw a dot for a speech sound written with a one-letter grapheme, e.g. bad
- draw a dash for a sound written with a two- or three-letter grapheme e.g. thing.
- draw a link to indicate a split grapheme, e.g. make.

Ask the children to add dots, dashes and links to the rest of the words in the list. Correct any errors with the children. Use this list to help you.

am and bad blot plan crib camp wind pond desk blend grunt

twist stiff press bluff thing spring drink this splash clutch slump

stretch spray boat tooth chair care more make spark sprain brute

bird spike law flight hair need join out read furl bloke stone tie

brown bow joy hear sure

Children can now move on to multi-syllabic words.

Tell the children that:
- The words in the box at the bottom of page 4 have more than one syllable.
- Explain that when we speak these words out loud the syllables often get squashed together, and so it is harder to know the speech sounds that are in the word.
- Point out that if we say these syllables very clearly and give them their 'full value' it makes spelling the words much easier. (The syllables in these words have been split in a way that makes it easy to say them out loud.)

Read the words and ask the children to repeat them (using the 'My turn, your turn' signal).
- Repeat saying each word, this time in full value syllables.

Show the children how to:
- draw a dot for a speech sound written with a one-letter grapheme
- draw a dash for a sound written with a two or three-letter grapheme
- draw a link to indicate a split grapheme e.g. a-e.

Ask the children to add dots, dashes and links to the rest of the words in the list, then correct any errors with their partners.

fo/ll ow   a/ddress   con/cen/trate   de/cide   a/lone   re/cog/nise   bo/rr ow

be/have   a/mount   croc/o/dile   ex/tra/va/gant   ac/cept/ance   dis/a/pp oint

com/pare   im/pa/tience   dis/grace/ful   be/cau se   aw/ful   ac/tion

23

Get Spelling! Introductory activities lesson plans

INTRODUCTORY ACTIVITY 4

Purpose: to assess children's knowledge of the alphabetic code

To help children voice what they have learnt so far about the alphabetic code, ask them to answer these questions with their partners:

- How many speech sounds are there in the English language?
- What do we call a letter or group of letters that we use to write down one speech sound?
- What are the most letters that can be used to spell one speech sound?
- What are the least number of letters?

Look at the spelling chart (see below). Ask the children how many different ways there are to spell each of these sounds:

/f/   /m/   /r/   /s/   /ay/   /igh/?

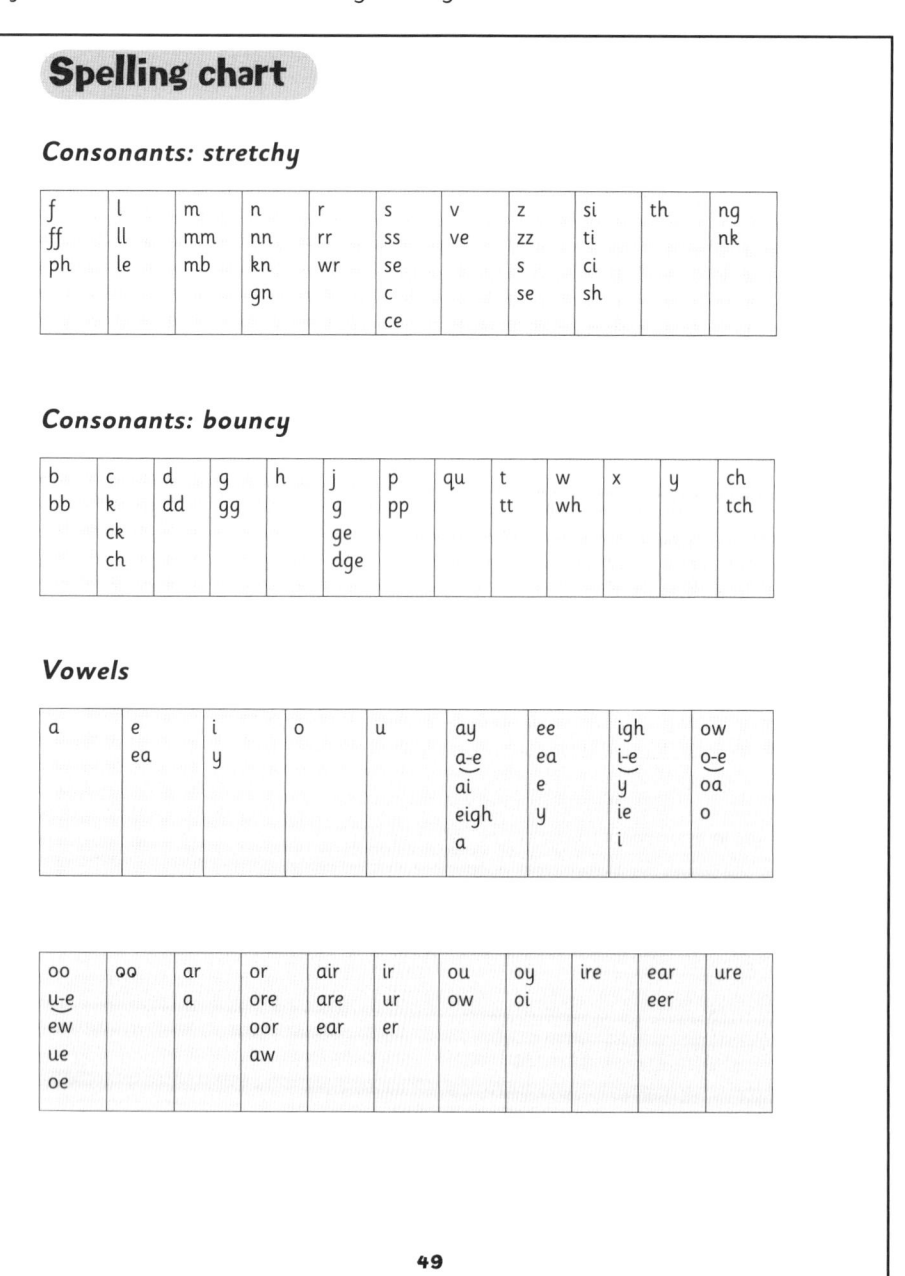

Spelling chart

Consonants: stretchy

f	l	m	n	r	s	v	z	si	th	ng
ff	ll	mm	nn	rr	ss	ve	zz	ti		nk
ph	le	mb	kn	wr	se		s	ci		
			gn		c		se	sh		
					ce					

Consonants: bouncy

b	c	d	g	h	j	p	qu	t	w	x	y	ch
bb	k	dd	gg		g	pp		tt	wh			tch
	ck				ge							
	ch				dge							

Vowels

a	e	i	o	u	ay	ee	igh	ow
	ea	y			a-e	ea	i-e	o-e
					ai	e	y	oa
					eigh	y	ie	o
					a		i	

oo	oo	ar	or	air	ir	ou	oy	ire	ear	ure
u-e		a	ore	are	ur	ow	oi		eer	
ew			oor	ear	er					
ue			aw							
oe										

49

This Spelling chart is on page 49 of each *Get Spelling! Book.*

Get Spelling! Introductory activities lesson plans

INTRODUCTORY ACTIVITY 5

Purpose: to help children find 'sounds' quickly on the spelling chart

Call out a few speech sounds from the spelling chart, asking children to point to the correct sound box as quickly as they can.

Once children can do this, ask the children, in pairs, to take turns calling out a sound while their partner points to it on the inside cover of their book.

INTRODUCTORY ACTIVITY 6

Purpose: to help children understand the difference between green and red words

Tell the children that there are two groups of words used in this spelling programme: red and green words.

- Green words are words that can be built using graphemes from the spelling chart. They are called 'green' words because you can spell and go!
- Red words are common usage words that include graphemes that are only found in those words and so they have not been included on the chart. They are called 'red' words because you have to stop and think how to spell them! These are words that children need to know thoroughly, e.g. 'said', 'does', 'though', 'through'.

Ask the children to work with a partner and circle the words that contain a grapheme that is not on the spelling chart. (The relevant words are in bold below.) Remind them that the grapheme may be on the chart but not for the sound in the word.

play   tree   dream   **would** (ou)   for   **your** (our)   that   **wh ere** (ere)   **said** (ai)   **kn ight**

world (or)   funny   **does** (oe)   **broth er** (o)   **son** (o)   sister

Get Spelling! Key activities example lesson plans

The eight spelling activities

Children need:
- *Read Write Inc. Get Spelling! Book 1, 2 or 3 Read Write Inc. Spelling Log Book*
- A spelling jotter
- A sharp pencil (do not use pens)
- A junior dictionary

The teacher needs:
- The spelling chart
- A white board and a pen
- A 'Red word' wall
- A 'Vocabulary wall' for new and interesting words

Once children have completed the introductory activities with you, they then complete the same eight key activities in each unit. Each unit in *Get Spelling! Book 1* focuses upon the spellings of one vowel speech sound. *Get Spelling! Book 2* focuses upon a new suffix combined with the words the children have learnt to spell in *Book 1*. *Get Spelling! Book 3* focuses upon key root words combined with all the suffixes the children have learnt in *Book 2*.

The same types of activities are used in all three books. This means that as the children progress through the programme you will spend less time explaining the activities and more time teaching children how to spell.

The plan below sets out a suggested order, but as you become familiar with the programme, there will be activities you will skip through quickly and others you may spend longer teaching, depending upon the children's knowledge and memory. Remember, some activities take longer while you and the children get into the swing of them.

Suggested schedule

10–15 minutes a day (Example for an 8 day per unit schedule)

Day 1 1: Information check 2: Dot, dash and count	**Day 5** 7: Dictation
Day 2 1: Information check 3: Write the root	**Day 6** 8: Spelling Log Plus a Two minute check
Day 3 1: Information check (quick) 4: Word fill 5: Circle the right one	**Review Day** (if needed) *Spelling Log Book* practice
Day 4 6: Four-in-a-row game	**Review Day** (if needed) *Spelling Log Book* practice

It is important that you are flexible in your use of the schedule. The timing in the above schedule is approximate. Some children may be able to work through each unit in a few days. It may be that some activities take longer and others less time, so an activity may need to continue on to the following day. You may also want to spend two days revising words in the children's *Spelling Log Books*.

Get Spelling! Key activities example lesson plans

Decide how many days children will spend on each unit and how much *Spelling Log Book* practice they need.

For example:
- Children with quick memories may only need:
  6 days per unit
- Children who make steady progress may need:
  8 days per unit
- Children who need a lot more practice may need:
  10 days per unit

1 Information check

Purpose: to introduce children to the words they will learn to spell over the week

Red words
Display the red words for the week with others that have been taught and practised on a 'Red word' wall.
Point and read these words with the children using the 'My turn, your turn' signal. Each set of words has a suggested idea how to help children learn them: mnemonics, words within words, 'naughty' letters, and spelling raps. Explanation for teaching these is in Appendix 2 on page 36. The words need to be taught and practised throughout the week and kept on display throughout the year until you know *all* your class *always* spells the word correctly in their own writing. You could perform a ceremony when a red word is taken off the wall!

Identify the graphemes (spellings) of the focus sound on the Spelling chart
Ask the children to look at the spelling chart on the back inside cover of their *Get Spelling!* books for the focus sound and identify the graphemes for that sound in the sound box. Ask them to count the number of different spellings.

Vocabulary check and homophones
There are a few words listed that may be outside some children's vocabulary. If the word is familiar pass on quickly to the next word.
Write the vocabulary words on the 'Vocabulary word' wall. Tell the children the meaning the first time you introduce the word, making your definition clear and to the point. It is better not to ask the children, because if they give a wrong definition this may cloud yours.
In some units homophones are included in the word lists, e.g. wait/weight; ate/eight. Write these words on the board and quickly tell the children the meaning of each word.

2 Dot, dash and count

Purpose: to help children match the speech sounds to graphemes

The grid lists words with different spellings for the key speech sound.

Get Spelling! Key activities example lesson plans

Show the children how to:
- dot the graphemes written with one letter
- dash the graphemes written with two or three letters
- draw a link to indicate a split grapheme, e.g. a-e, i-e, o-e
- add up the total number of speech sounds in each word and write the number in the next column.

(N.B. The answers for the words in each grid are provided on page 45 onwards.)

Then ask the children to fill in the boxes on their own and then to make sure they have the same number of speech sounds as their partner.

Explain the Spelling Tip, if there is one, e.g. "'ay' always comes at the end of a root word – never in the middle."

③ Write the root/suffix

Purpose: to help children to spell the root of the word with the following suffixes: 'ed', 'ing', 's', 'es', 'y', 'ly', 'er, 'est', 'iest'.

Explain that many words are often made from a 'root' word, e.g.
    jump: **jump**ing, **jump**ed, **jump**s, **jump**er
    run: **run**ning, **run**s, **run**ner

The root gives the most meaning to a word. The suffix is a word-ending that is added to a root word to give more information about the root word, e.g.
    jump + ing = jump**ing**
    run(+ n) + er = runn**er**

Explain how the root word is affected by the suffix.

Use the spelling tip (if there is one included) to explain how a particular suffix changes the spelling of a root word, e.g. when the suffix 'ing' is added to words ending in 'e' (make, like, escape) the 'e' is dropped: "You can't have an E with an I-N-G!" Remind children to put back 'e' when the root is written alone.

A list of the suffixes taught is in Appendix 3 on page 38.

The suffix shows how a word will be used within the sentence and what part of speech the word belongs to – that is whether it is a noun, verb, adjective or an adverb.

The root part of the word can stand on its own as a word, e.g. 'jump', but a suffix cannot, e.g. 'ing'. Show the children how to decide which part of the word is the root and which is the suffix, and where to write the root word or the suffix in their *Get Spelling! Books*.

N.B. In *Get Spelling! Book 3* you will need to guide the children closely with this activity as some root words change their spelling when a suffix or prefix is added, e.g. – describe + -tion: description.

Get Spelling! Key activities example lesson plans

④ Word fill (partner assessment)

Purpose: to help children select the correct spelling or homophone so a sentence makes sense

Before the children start this activity, you may need to read through the sentence with them. Make sure they remember the meanings of the homophones discussed during the *Information check* activity.

Show the children how to work with partners to:
- select the correct word to write in each space
- check that both of them have selected the same words.

Check the children's answers and correct any errors with them.

⑤ Circle the right one (partner assessment)

Purpose: to help children select the correct spelling from two other incorrect spellings of the same word

Show the children how to work with partners to:
- circle the correct spelling in each row
- check they both have the same answers
- check their answers in their dictionary.

You will need to teach children how to find words quickly in a dictionary. This could be taught in a different lesson.

⑥ Four-in-a row game (partner assessment)

Purpose: to help children recall the spellings of words practised

This game is a way for children to practise the spellings of words they have encountered in the unit over the last few days.

Show the children how to work together with a partner to complete this activity.

Partner 1s:
- choose any word from Activity 2 (Dot, dash and count) and 3 (Write the root/suffix) lists, that they think will challenge their partner
- ask their partner to write the word in a jotter (without their partner looking at the word in the list)
- tick the circle (or diamond or triangle) in their partner's *Get Spelling! Book* if it is correct. If it isn't, children correct the part of their partner's word that is wrong.

Partners then swap roles after each word. The winner is the first to spell four words in a row correctly.

Get Spelling! Key activities example lesson plans

7 Dictation (partner assessment)

Purpose: to help children recall the spellings within a sentence

This activity provides further practice for children to spell words they have encountered in the unit, but this time within the context of a sentence.

Show children how to complete this dictation activity with a partner.
Partner 1s:
- read aloud for their partner the first sentence from Unit 1 dictation sentences (for Partner 2) at the back of the *Get Spelling! Books*.
- watch carefully as their partner writes the sentence in a jotter.
- tick each word in their partner's jotter if correct, or, if not, corrects the part of the word that is wrong.

Partners then swap roles after each sentence, using the Partner 1 and 2 sentences.

There are extra dictation sentences for more able children or for extra practice in Appendix 4 on page 39.

8 Spelling Log (individual assessment)

Purpose: to help children identify words with difficult parts

Children are more likely to remember how to spell a word when they explain why it is difficult to their partner.

Both partners choose five words from the lists in activities 2 and 3 (in *Get Spelling! Book 3* they will need to choose from activity 3) that they have found the most challenging, and then write them in their grid in *Spelling Log Book* page for that unit.

Show them how to circle the part of the word they find most difficult to remember and to explain to their partner why this is so. Partners take turns to discuss how they will remember how to spell their chosen words, e.g. by exaggerating the pronunciation, drawing the difficult letter/s larger or by saying the difficult letters louder. Avoid asking children to decide too many mnemonics as these can be easy to forget later.

Children then take it turns to call out their partner's set of five words to see how quickly their partner can write them down. They then correct their partner's spellings.

These are the words that children should now take home to practise. Parents could be asked to review five new and five old words each week including two red words. The parent calls out the words and every time the child spells the word correctly the parent writes the date and their initials next to the word in the Log.

Get Spelling! Key activities example lesson plans

Two minute check

Purpose: to help children review words from previous units
This can be used for group and individual assessment.
Select five words from previous pages in the children's *Spelling Log* books or from common errors in their own writing books. Write these on the board, including the error, alongside five other correctly spelled words you have taught.
Give children one minute to decide which five words are spelt incorrectly and to write them correctly.
Give partners one more minute to check the answers with their partner.
Select children to feed back their answers to the class.

Marking and assessing children's work

It is important that children are encouraged to write freely when they are writing their own compositions. If too much pressure is put on children to spell correctly, they will select words that they can spell rather than more exciting or appropriate words they cannot.

Mark children's compositions for the quality of the ideas and use of language. These comments should be discussed with children before discussing punctuation and spelling.

- Underline, lightly, in pencil, common errors they will be likely to correct quickly without a dictionary.
- Underline, more heavily, repeated errors, which you *really* want them to spell correctly!
- Put a wavy line under exciting words and, if spelt incorrectly, write the correct spelling lightly in pencil, praising them for having made such a fabulous attempt at such an adventurous word! Do not ask them to correct it themselves by looking in a dictionary - you may put them off using good words!

Keep your own spelling log of common errors that children are making. Make a mark against misspelt words that have been taught in the spelling lessons, to remind you to review this unit. Include the common errors in the *Two minute check* activity.

Appendix 1 Photocopiable Introductory Activities

The following four pages contain the *Get Spelling! Book 1* introductory activities and can be used with children who have not done *Book 1* of this series, to introduce the English alphabetic code.

Introductory activities

> Do these activities before you start. Your teacher will take you through the activities to give you a strong framework for the whole spelling programme.

Activity 1

When we speak we use 44 speech sounds. All the words in English are made up of just 44 sounds. There are about 24 consonant speech sounds and 20 vowel speech sounds.

The consonant speech sounds

Some of the consonant speech sounds can be stretched and others can be bounced.

★ Say the stretched speech sounds below, taking turns with your partner. Make sure you do not say *uh* at the end of each sound (*lllll* not *luh*; *mmmm* not *muh*; *nnnn* not *nuh*, *ffff* not *fuh*; *ssss* not *suh*; *shhhh* not *shuh*)

f	l	m	n	r	s	v	z	sh	th	th	ng nk

★ Say the bounced speech sounds below, taking turns with your partner. Make sure you do not say *uh*; *b* not *buh*; *c* not *cuh*
(The two boxes with ! in, are really two speech sounds said at the same time. Say them quickly and count them as one.)

b	c	d	g	j	p	qu !	t	w	x !	y	ch

The vowel speech sounds

★ With your partner, take turns saying these sounds to each other.

a apple	e egg	i insect	o orange	u umbrella	ay play	ee see	igh high	ow blow	oo zoo
oo look	ar car	or for	air fair	ir girl	ou shout	oy boy	ire fire	ear hear	ure pure

32

2

© Oxford University Press 2008. This page may be reproduced for use solely within the purchaser's school or college.

Appendix 1 Photocopiable Introductory Activities

Activity 2

There is one speech sound in each sound box. Each word in the list below has one grapheme written in bold, e.g. **ph**oto.

- ★ Read and say the word '**ph**oto'.
- ★ Say the grapheme '**ph**' (letter names).
- ★ Say the *f* speech sound and write '**ph**' in the box.
- ★ Repeat with each word.

photo hu**ff** be**ll** la**mb** autu**mn** **kn**ow **gn**aw
fu**nn**y **wr**ap ca**rr**y **c**ircus pa**ss** pie**ce** gi**ve** bu**zz**
wa**s** **c**aution spe**ci**al

f	l	m	n	r	s	v	z	sh	th	th	ng

ru**bb**le **d**u**ck** **ch**emist da**dd**y gi**gg**le **g**erm
ju**dge** bar**ge** ha**pp**y bo**tt**le **wh**ich ca**t**ch

b	c	d	g	j	p	qu	t	w	x	y	ch

h**ea**d g**y**m m**a**ke tr**ai**n dr**ea**m ha**pp**y k**i**te
t**ie** b**y** sm**o**ke t**oe** g**o** bl**ue** ch**ew** p**u**t f**a**ther
sn**o**re p**oo**r l**aw** **au**thor b**ur**n h**er** br**ow**n
sp**oi**l d**ee**r h**ear** c**are** advent**ure**

a apple	e egg	i insect	o orange	u umbrella	ay play	ee see	igh high	ow snow	oo zoo
oo book	ar car	or for	air fair	ir girl	ou shout	oy boy	ire fire	ear hear	ure pure

Appendix I Photocopiable Introductory Activities

Activity 3

★ Take turns, with your partner to say each word below in speech sounds.
★ Draw a dot for a speech sound written with a one-letter grapheme, e.g. bad.
★ Draw a dash for a sound written with a two or three-letter grapheme, e.g. thing, light.
★ Draw a link to indicate a split grapheme, e.g. make.

am and bad blot plan crib camp wind pond desk blend grunt

twist stiff press bluff thing spring drink this splash clutch slump

stretch spray boat tooth chair care more make spark sprain brute

bird spike law flight hair need join out read furl bloke stone tie

brown bow joy hear sure

The words below have more than one syllable. When we speak these words out loud the syllables often get squashed together and so it is harder to know the speech sounds that are in the word. If we say these syllables very clearly and give them their 'full value' it makes spelling much easier.

★ Say each word in full value syllables.
★ Draw a dot for a speech sound written with a one-letter grapheme.
★ Draw a dash for a sound written with a two or three-letter grapheme.
★ Draw a link to indicate a split grapheme, e.g. re/place.

fo/llow a/ddress con/cen/trate de/cide a/lone re/cog/nise bo/rrow

be/have a/mount croc/o/dile ex/tra/vag/ant ac/cept/ance dis/a/ppoint

com/pare im/pa/tience dis/grace/ful be/cause aw/ful ac/tion

Appendix I Photocopiable Introductory Activities

Activity 4

★ Complete these questions with your partner.

1. How many speech sounds are there in the English language? _____
2. What do we call a letter or group of letters that we use to write down one speech sound? _____
3. What are the most letters that can be used to spell one speech sound? _____
4. What are the least number of letters? _____
5. How many different ways are there to spell the sound:

   f _____ m _____ r _____ s _____ ay _____ igh _____?

Activity 5

★ Call out a speech sound from the spelling chart on page 49 – see how quickly your partner can point to the correct sound box.

Activity 6

There are two groups of words used in this spelling programme: red and green words.

Green words are words that can be built using graphemes from the spelling chart. They are called 'green' words because you can spell and go!

Red words are common words that include a grapheme that is not on the spelling chart on page 49. They are called 'red' words because you have to stop and think how to spell them!

The words below are split into graphemes.
With your partner, circle the eight words that contain a grapheme that is not on the spelling chart for that particular sound. These are red words.

> p-l-ay t-r-ee d-r-ea-m w-oul-d f-or y-our th-a-t wh-ere
> s-ai-d kn-igh-t w-or-l-d f-u-nn-y d-oe-s b-r-o-th-er s-o-n s-i-s-t-er

5

Appendix 2 Red Word activities

The following activities are suggested as ways of learning red words. The activity type is always noted next to the red words in the Information check boxes in *Get Spelling! Book 1*.

Mnemonics

Use the phrase to help the children learn the tricky bit of the word, or you can help the children to think of their own shared mnemonic:

w**ould**, c**ould**, sh**ould** sh**ould**er: o *(oh)* u *(you)* lovely darling
r**ough**, en**ough**, th**ough**, th**ough**t, b**ough**t: o *(oh)* u *(you)* great hooligan
c**augh**t, d**augh**ter, n**augh**ty, l**augh**: a *(eh)* u *(you)* great hooligan
s**ai**d: *its got an A and an I and I don't know why*
because: *big elephants can't always use small entrances* Draw an illustration and label this phrase.

e.g. For 'would, could, should shoulder' (tricky bit: ould):
- Write the word on the white board.
- Say the word: 'would'.
- Say the spelling in letter names: W-O-U-L-D, but read out the tricky bit in a silly voice: O-U-L-D
- Say 'o (oh) u (you) lovely darling' in a silly voice.
- Say the whole spelling again.

Repeat this method with the other words.
Rub the words off the board.
Ask the children to write the word as they say the spelling out loud, in whispers, then silently.
N.B. Don't use too many mnemonics; sometimes it is easier to remember the word than the mnemonic.

Say it as it looks

Simply pronounce the word in a silly voice by the way it looks and then as we say it normally.

wh**a**t w**a**tch w**a**s (say *a* as in apple)
pr**e**tty (say *e* as in egg)
T**w**o as in t**w**in (twoh)
D**oe**s and d**oe**sn't (say *oe* as in toe)
My m**o**ther had an**o**ther br**o**ther (say *o* as in hot) Draw an illustration and label this phrase.

e.g. For 'what watch was':
- Write the word on the white board.
- Say the word: what (say *a* as in apple).
- Say the word within a sentence: "What (as in apple) do you think you're doing?"
Repeat this method with the other words.

Rub the words off the board.
Ask the children to write the word as they say the word out loud.

Word in a word

That's **one** thing I have g**one** and d**one**
business on the **bus**
It's **bus**y on the **bus**
or in w**or**k w**or**d w**or**se
ear in l**ear**n **ear**th h**ear**t

our in y**our** and f**our**
me in co**me** and so**me**
all in sm**all** b**all** t**all**
any in m**any**

Appendix 2 Red Word activities

e.g. For 'It's busy on the bus':
- Write the sentence on the white board.
- Say the phrase: 'It's busy on the bus' (say 'bussy' not 'bizzy').
- Say the spelling in letter names: B-U-S but say U in a silly voice.

Repeat this method with the other words.

Rub the words off the board.
Ask the children to write the word as they say the spelling out loud, in whispers, then silently.

A naughty letter

These words are often spelled incorrectly because of one unexpected or 'naughty' letter.
Write the word with the naughty letter really big and then draw something helpful in the shape of the letter, e.g.

o in pe**o**ple: draw a face
i in fr**i**end: draw your friend - dot for the head, stick for the body
i in ju**i**cy fruit: draw a lolly or fruit in the shape of i
u in b**u**ild: draw a house inside u
l in wa**l**k and ta**l**k: draw yourself on one 'l' your friend on the other 'l'.
u in bisc**u**it: draw half a biscuit in u
o in y**o**ung: draw a baby in its cot inside o
w in **w**ho: draw a worm on w

e.g. For 'people':
- Write the word on the white board.
- Say the word: 'people'.
- Ask the children which is the naughty letter that has escaped into the word (o).
- Draw a picture of a face inside o.
- Say the spelling in letter names: P-E-O-P-LE but say **O** in a cross voice, as though telling off the letter.

Repeat this method with the other words.

Rub the words off the board.
Ask the children to write the word as they say the spelling out loud, in whispers, then silently.

Rap it

Say the word, then the graphemes in a rhythm and then repeat the word again, e.g.

Where - WH - ERE - where   *or*   There - TH - ERE - there   *or*   Were - W- ERE - were

e.g. For 'where':
- Write the word on the white board.
- Say the word: 'where'.
- Say the spelling in letter names: WH-ERE.
- Develop a rap rhythm with attitude, as you say the letter names: <u>WH</u> - <u>ERE</u>

Repeat this method with the other words.

Rub the words off the board.
Ask the children to write the word as they say the spelling out loud, in whispers, then silently.

Appendix 3 Roots and Suffixes

'ed'
This ending is pronounced in three ways: 'id' as in landed, 't' as in jumped and 'd' as in saved. 'e' in save doubles up when 'ed' is added, e.g. saved.

'ing'
Watch out when you add 'ing' to verbs ending with 'e', e.g. like, hate, love.
Say "You can't have an 'E' with an 'I-N-G'", e.g.
liking, hating, loving.
Exception: 'ageing': 'e' remains to keep the 'g' saying 'j'.

's'/'es'
You need to add 'es' after a word ending in 's', 'z', 'sh' or 'ch', e.g. churches, passes, pushes.
When 's' is added to a word ending in 'y', the 'y' changes to 'ie'. e.g.
lady - ladies   baby - babies

'y'
"Drop the E when you add a Y", e.g.
shine - shiny   whine - whiny
slime - slimy

'er' and 'est'
'Y' changes to 'I', e.g.
happy - happier, happiest   slimy - slimier - slimiest
shiny - shinier - shiniest

Double letters
In most short words ending in a one-letter consonant, you need to double the last letter when you add a suffix – but only when the vowel is a short vowel sound, e.g.

    'a' in clap: clapping, clapped   'o' in hop: hopping, popped, stopper
    'e' in let: letting, letter, lesser   'u' in hug: hugging, tugged, rudder
    'i' in sit: hitting, litter, 'fittest

You also need to double the last consonant letter in longer words too – but only where the stress is on the last syllable, e.g.
travel - travelling, travelled, traveller
begin - beginning, beginner
kidnap - kidnapping, kidnapped, kidnapper

Appendix 4 Extra dictation sentences

Book 1

The following dictation sentences are different from those in the *Get Spelling! Books*. These provide:
- extra practice for children to return to
- or extra challenge for more able children.

Unit 1
Wait for the delayed train.
They gave him a birthday cake.
Explain how you made the mistake.
Do not make a mistake.

Unit 2
Leave me to eat in peace.
Please feel free to disagree.
I need to speak please.
I only need three more sweets.

Unit 3
I like writing to my grandad.
I might decide to try my big bike.
Give me a nice wide smile.
Why are you so polite tonight?

Unit 4
Who knows the road to follow?
Who moans the most in the class?
I'm home alone with no telephone.
A goat on a boat is no joke.

Unit 5
Rescue my shoe from the pool.
Who has the newest boots?
I knew that you were chewing.
Shoot to school on a blue scooter.

Unit 6
I found a brown mouse in our house.
We shouted out the loudest at the match.
Ouch: a mouse ran down my trousers.
He went to town without a sound.

Appendix 4 Extra dictation sentences

Unit 7
Don't play in the park at dark.
The artist went to a garden party.
I lost my glasses in the classroom.
A fast car whizzed past the starting mark.

Unit 8
My hamster whirls and twirls on the wheel.
I squirmed as she nursed my burn.
The girl was first to get to the church.
The birds were turning and twirling.

Unit 9
Beware of the bear, he said in despair.
Have you a spare pair of chairs?
What's the fare to the airport?
Which one is the hairiest fairy?

Unit 10
Crawl on the floor to the wall.
What sort of horse is in the story?
You will fall off the tall wall.
He crawled under the door to get the ball.

Unit 11
Point to the noisiest boy in the room.
I enjoyed the choice of toys.
Please stop annoying the boys.
I was disappointed by all the noise.

Unit 12
The bonfire was as tall as a church spire.
Hear the cheer as the fireworks fly.
My grandad retired last year.
I require you to come here now.

Appendix 4 Extra dictation sentences

Book 2

The following dictation sentences are different from those in the *Get Spelling! Books*. These provide:
- extra practice for children to return to
- or extra challenge for more able children.

Unit 1
You need space to keep a bicycle.
The ice-cream is excellent.
I will certainly come to the circus.
Your racer bicycle is very nice.

Unit 2
I have an urgent message for you.
Cutting tall hedges can be dangerous.
I keep my carriage in a garage.
Are giraffes gentle animals?

Unit 3
My cat has nine lives.
Buy your tomatoes and potatoes here.
The leaves fall from the trees.
Keep away from those knives.

Unit 4
I have travelled many miles.
The baby is just beginning to crawl.
The clapping inspired me to sing louder.
I am planning an exciting holiday.

Unit 5
I love cuddling my large ginger cat.
Stop giggling through the concert.
Please take care when handling the kittens.
How many angles in a triangle?

Unit 6
I usually walk to school.
Please work individually today.
Divide the sweets equally.
Are you identical twins?

Appendix 4 Extra dictation sentences

Unit 7
I ironed all my own shirts.
The policeman questioned the man all night.
Suddenly, the sky lit up with fireworks.
She listened carefully as the teacher talked.

Unit 8
We had a discussion about education.
In which direction are you heading?
You have a wild imagination.
How many relations do you have?

Unit 9
Laws are made by the government.
You must learn to be patient.
I train my dog to be obedient.
She looked at me in amazement.

Unit 10
What is the distance to your home?
Your absence from school is stopping you learn.
Silence is required during assembly.
You need patience to be a teacher.

Unit 11
It is dangerous to climb on the bridge.
Dad looks ridiculous when he dances.
Be generous and share your sweets.
You must be cautious as you cross the road.

Unit 12
Your behaviour makes me very proud.
The pirates captured the sailing boat.
I am terrified of spiders.
My sister loves colouring in pictures.

Unit 13
My new sofa is very comfortable.
My sister is very knowledgeable about computers.
Your clothes are unsuitable for school.
Please try to be reasonable to your mother.

Unit 14
The princess was famous for being beautiful.
Hopefully, I will go on holiday this year.
Jack is a skilful and adventurous cook.
Was Gita successful in passing the exam?

Appendix 4 Extra dictation sentences

Book 3

The following dictation sentences are different from those in the *Get Spelling! Books*. These provide:
- extra practice for children to return to
- or extra challenge for more able children.

Unit 1
I love adventurous sports.
I accidentally spilled your coffee.
I am full of admiration for my sister.
The hotel had run out of accommodation.

Unit 2
I am writing to show my appreciation of your kindness.
My dog is so affectionate to me.
Mum's keys are always disappearing.
His appearance shocked us all.

Unit 3
I am tall in comparison to my mum.
Peter does not enjoy competitions.
I have finally completed my homework.
You can't play on your computer all night.

Unit 4
I concentrated very hard in the maths lesson.
The queue for the match continued all round the stadium.
Congratulations on your tenth birthday.
He was barely conscious after falling off his bike.

Unit 5
Your lying does not deceive me.
Have you made your decision yet?
I am determined to be a footballer.
The description of the hotel sounds lovely.

Unit 6
My brother always exaggerates his stories.
I was exhausted after climbing the mountain.
I hope you have a good explanation for me.
Your poem is really excellent.

Appendix 4 Extra dictation sentences

Unit 7
I am writing about an imaginary forest.
Everyone must report to me immediately.
You need intelligence to become an astronaut.
The book had beautiful illustrations.

Unit 8
My teacher is producing the school play.
We provided a lovely tea for the visitors.
Everyone looked very presentable for the party.
Accidents are usually preventable.

Unit 9
Who is responsible for this mess?
The chorus is repeated ten times.
Where do your relations live?
It is your responsibility to empty the bins.

Unit 10
There was chaos in the chemist at lunchtime.
Everyone in school had stomach ache.
I play the main character in the school play.
I play in the orchestra and sing in the choir.

Unit 11
I photographed elephants in India.
We lost the match; it was a catastrophe!
A pharmacist works in a chemist.
We were triumphant; our team was successful.

Unit 12
The unique view was picturesque.
My team is in the premier league.
The monster's face was grotesque.
I found a unique chair in the antique shop.

Appendix 5 Answers: *Get Spelling! Book 1*

Answers to Activity 2 Dot dash and count

Unit 1 'ay'

day 2, way 2, away 3, stray 4, delay 4, today 4, Monday 5, holiday 6, birthday 5,

made 3, ate 2, make 3, take 3, came 3, gave 3, save 3, brave 4, date 3, cage 3, escape 5,

mistake 6, chocolate 7,

wait 3, paid 3, pain 3, train 4, rain 3, fail 3, afraid 5, complain 7, explain 6,

weight 3, eight 2, weigh 2, apron 5, table 4, able 3

Unit 2 'ee'

see 2, tree 3, three 3, week 3, need 3, feed 3, feel 3, sleep 4, agree 4, disagree 7, indeed 5,

between 6, thirteen 5, fourteen 5, eighteen 4, nineteen 6,

sea 2, tea 2, speak 4, weak 3, real 3, leave 3, each 2, teach 3, read 3, peace 3, please 4,

beautiful 8

he 2, we 2, me 2, she 2, happy 4, ugly 4, only 4, body 4

Unit 3 'igh'

high 2, night 3, light 3, bright 4, fight 3, might 3, right 3, tonight 5, sigh 2

like 3, hide 3, wide 3, time 3, mine 3, nice 3, mice 3, slice 4, side 3, write 3, quite 3, smile 4,

decide 5, beside 5, polite 5, recognise 8

by 2, my 2, try 3, fly 3, why 2, sky 3, reply 5, find 4, kind 4, mind 4, child 4

Unit 4 'ow'

know 2, knows 3, snow 3, throw 3, blow 3, grow 3, show 2, bowl 3, borrow 4, follow 4,

pillow 4, tomorrow 6,

broke 4, choke 3, smoke 4, whole 3, hole 3, rode 3, hope 3, note 3, nose 3, wrote 3, stone 4,

alone 4, telephone 7

boat 3, coat 3, float 4, road 3, goat 3, moan 3, groan 4, so 2, go 2, no 2, most 4

Unit 5 'oo'

too 2, zoo 2, school 4, room 3, soon 3, moon 3, spoon 4, tooth 3, root 3, shoo 2,

flute 4, brute 4, cute 3,

blew 3, new 2, knew 2, threw 3, grew 3, flew 3, view 3, few 2,

blue 3, true 3, rescue 5, continue 7, statue 5, argue 3,

to 2, two 2, onto 4, who 2, shoe 2

45

Appendix 5 Answers: *Get Spelling! Book 1*

Unit 6 'ou'

loud 2, out 2, sh out 3, about 4, hou se 3, mou se 3, found 4, sound 4, ground 5, ours 3, mound 4, our 2, (h)our 2, with out 5, amount 5, around 5, trousers 6, flour 3, (h)ours 3, cow 2, now 2, how 2, down 3, town 3, brown 4, frown 4, drown 4, flower 4, sh ower 3, tower 3

Unit 7 'ar'

car 2, bar 2, far 2, star 3, arm 2, harm 3, ch arm 3, farm 3, start 4, sh arp 3, park 3, dark 3, sh ark 3, lar ge 3, remark 5, artist 5, garden 5, party 4

grass 4, glass 4, class 4, fast 3, mast 3, last 3, graph 4, plant 5, path 3

Unit 8 'ir'

girl 3, skirt 4, sh irt 3, dirt 3, bird 3, th ird 3, first 4, wh irl 3, twirl 4, firm 3, squ irm 4

hurt 3, burn 3, turn 3, nur se 3, pur se 3, ch ur ch 3

her 2, lett er 4, bett er 4, wett er 4, hamster 6, butt er 4

Unit 9 'air'

air 1, ch air 2, pair 2, stair 3, fair 2, repair 4, airport 4, despair 5

squ are 3, sh are 2, care 2, stare 3, bare 2, fare 2, declare 5, aware 3, beware 4, compare 5, rare 2, spare 3

wear 2, bear 2, pear 2

Unit 10 'or'

for 2, more 2, fork 3, storm 4, hor se 3, born 3, sort 3, sore 2, store 3, story 4, adore 3

door 2, poor 2, floor 3, indoor 4

saw 2, jaw 2, draw 3, paw 2, crawl 4, awful 4

Unit 11 'oy'

boy 2, toy 2, joy 2, enjoy 4, employ 5, destroy 6, ann oy 3

boil 3, spoil 4, ch oi ce 3, voi ce 3, noi se 3, point 4, join 3, foil 3, toilet 5, disapp oint 8

Unit 12 'ear' 'ire'

hear 2, dear 2, fear 2, spear 3

cheer 2, deer 2

here 2

fire 2, spire 3, hire 2, wire 2, inspire 5, admire 4, retire 4, requ ire 4

Appendix 5 Answers: *Get Spelling! Book 2*

Answers to Activity 2 Dot dash and count
The answers below are for the words pronounced with full value syllables.

Unit 1 soft 'c'

city 4, cir-cus 5, cer-tain 5, ce-re-al 6, bi-cycle 6, cent(re) 5, cycle 4

ice 2, nice 3, rice 3, lice 3, mice 3, price 4, twice 4, off-ice 4, po-l-ice 5

ace 2, face 3, race 3, lace 3, space 4

ex-cell-ent 8, ex-cept 6, con-cert 6, con-cen-trate 10

Unit 2 soft 'g'

gen-er-al 6, giraffe 5, gentle 5, age 2, angel 5, urgent 5, danger 5, lar ge 3, fringe 5,

plunge 5, strange 6, orange 5, bridge 4, ridge 3, wedge 3, hedge 3, pledge 4, judge 3,

marri-age 6, ga-rage 5, garb-age 5, cabb-age 5, mass-age 5, cott-age 5, vill-age 5

Unit 3 Unusual plurals

baby 4, tomato 6, potato 6, wolf 4, shelf 4, life 3, knife 3, leaf 3, woman 5, sh eep 3, lady 4,

loaf 4

Unit 4 Short vowel doubling

flap 4, clap 4, get 3, stamp 5, stick 4, strand 6, plan 4, spin 4, grin 4, hug 3, slim 4, kidnap 6,

jetlag 6, worship 5, travel 6, begin 5

Unit 5 '-le'

midd le 4, app le 4, litt le 4, cudd le 4, battle 4, puzz le 4, gigg le 4, kett le 4, candle 5, simple 5,

handle 5, angle 4, whis(t)le 4, triangle 7, rectangle 8

Unit 6 '-al' '-il' '-el'

pu-pil 5, A-pril 5, pen-cil 6, an-gel 5, jew-el 4, med-al 5, us-u-al 5, grad-u-al 7,

i-den-ti-cal 9, roy-al 4, e-qu al 4, in-div-i-du-al 10, med-i-cal 7, trad-i-tion-al 10

Unit 7 '-en' '-on' '-an' '-in'

gar-den 5, o-pen 4, hidd-en 5, sudd-en 5, list-en 6, wo-man 5, or-phan 4, cou-sin 5, i-ron 4,

drag-on 6, reas-on 5, o-pin-i-on 6, on-i-on 5, less-on 5, butt-on 5, rel-i-g-i-on 8

Appendix 5 Answers: *Get Spelling! Book 2*

Unit 8 '-tion' '-sion'

ac-tion 6, in-fec-tion 8, op-er-a-tion 7, con-cen-tra-tion 12, add-i-tion 6, a-ffec-tion 7, sub-trac-tion 10, cel-e-bra-tion 10, punc-tu-a-tion 10, di-rec-tion 8, re-la-tion 7, ed-u-ca-tion 7, i-mag-i-na-tion 10 pro-gress-ion 10, con-fess-ion 9, po-ssess-ion 8, dis-cuss-ion 9, re-vi-sion 7, tel-e-vi-sion 9, de-ci-sion 7, di-vi-sion 7, ex-plo-sion 8

Unit 9 '-ent' '-ant' '-ment'

par-ent 5, an-cient 6, de-pend-ent 9, vi-o-lent 7, ur-gent 5, ac-cid-ent 8, in-de-pen-dent 11, pa-tient 6, o-be-di-ent 8, ab-sent 6

dis-tant 7, con-stant 8, im-por-tant 8, ser-vant 6, gi-ant 5, el-e-gant 7, ex-trava-gant 11

treat-ment 8, judge-ment 7, ar-gu-ment 7, de-part-ment 9, en-joy-ment 8, gov-ern-ment 9, a-maze-ment 8, ex-per-i-ment 9

Unit 10 '-ence' '-ance'

pa-tience 6, im-pa-tience 8, vi-o-lence 7, ab-sence 6, si-lence 6, de-pen-dence 9, in-de-pen-dence 11, o-be-di-ence 8 dis-tance 7, im-por-tance 8, ex-tra-va-gance 11, el-e-gance 7

Unit 11 '-ous' '-cious' '-tious'

fa-mous 5, gor-geous 5, jeal-ous 5, ner-vous 5, e-nor-mous 6, ri-dic-u-lous 9, se-ri-ous 6, fu-ri-ous 6, cu-ri-ous 6, re-li-gi-ous 8, cour-age-ous 6, dan-ger-ous 7, gen-er-ous 6, de-li-cious 7, pre-ci ous 6, am-bi-ti ous 8, cau-ti ous 5

Unit 12 Schwa: '-ure' '-or' '-our'

na-ture 4, pic-ture 4, mix-ture 5, ad-ven-ture 7, temp-er-a-ture 8, fur-ni-ture 6, cap-ture 5, lit-er-a-ture 7, trea-sure 5, plea-sure 5, in-jure 4, fail-ure 4, te-rr or 4, mi-rr or 4, be-hav-i-our 7, col-our 4

Unit 13 '-ible' '-ibly' '-able' '-ably'

man-age 5, val-ue 4, like 3, com-fort 6, rea-son 5, ar-gue 3, kn ow 2, kn ow-ledge 5, suit 3

Unit 14 '-ful' '-fully'

care 2, ch eer 2, thank 3, hope 3, th ought 3, pea ce 3, pur-pose 5, skill 4, suc-cess 6, de-light 5, won-der 4, col-our 4, bea-u-ty 5

48

Appendix 5 Answers: *Get Spelling! Book 3*

Answers to Activity 2 Dot dash and count
The answers below are for the words pronounced with full value syllables.

Unit 1 '-ac' '-ad'
ac-cept 6, ac-cid-ent 8, ac-com-o-date 9, ad-mire 4, ad-dress 6, ad-ven-ture 7

Unit 2 '-a'
a-ffect 5, a-ttract 6, a-ppear 3, a-ppre-ci-ate 8, a-pp oint 5, a-gree 4

Unit 3 'com-'
com-pare 5, com-pete 6, com-plain 7, com-plete 7, com-pute 6

Unit 4 'con-'
con-cen-trate 10, con-grat-u-late 11, con-scious 6, con-science 7, con-tin-ue 7

Unit 5 'de-' 'dis-'
de-ceive 5, de-cide 5, de-termine 7, de-pend 6, des-cribe 7, dis-cuss 6

Unit 6 'ed-' 'ex-'
ed-u-cate 6, ex-agg-er-ate 7, ex-cel 5, ex-cept 6, ex-cite 5, ex-haust 6, ex-plain 6

Unit 7 'il-' 'im-' 'in-'
ill-us-trate 8, i-mag-ine 6, im-port-ant 8, in-tell-i-gent 10

Unit 8 'pre' 'pro'
pre-pare 5, pre-tend 7, pre-vent 7, pres-ent 7, pro-duce 6, pro-vide 6

Unit 9 're'
re-peat 5, re-move 5, re-fuse 5, re-late 5, re-spons-ible 10

Unit 10 'ch' = k, sh
'ch' making k   chemist 7, cha-os 4, ache 2, tech-nic-al 8, scheme 4, cha-rac-ter 7,

kn ow-ledge 5, sch ool 4, ech-o 3, mech-an-i-cal 9, choir 2, stom-ach 6, orch-es-tra 7, arch-i-tect 7

'ch' making sh   ma-chine 5, pa-ra-chute 7, bro-chure 5, sched-ule 5

Unit 11 'ph' = *f*
physic-al 7, para-graph 8, photo-graph 8, alpha-bet 7, el-e-phant 7, tri-umph 6

phrase 3, sphere 3, or-phan 4, pharm-a-cy 6, geo-graphy 8, neph-ew 4, cat-as-trophe 10

Unit 12 '-que' = *k* '-gue' = *g*
antique 5, cheque 3, unique 4, picturesque 8, grotesque 7, fatigue 5, prologue 6, lea gue 3,

coll ea gue 5, catalogue 7

Appendix 6 Word banks

Get Spelling! Book 1
Below are further examples of words containing the graphemes focussed on in the *Get Spelling! Book 1* units.

Unit 1 'ay'
ay

| clay | display | hurray | pay | spray | sway | yesterday |
| decay | hay | lay | pray | stay | tray | |

a–e

ace	brake	educate	enrage	shake	stage	
awake	crave	estate	lace	shame	tame	
became	create	fake	operate	shave	teenage	
behave	date	fame	pace	slate	trace	
blame	debate	fate	place	slave	wake	
brace	drake	frame	quake	space	wave	

ai

| bait | complaint | rail | saint | wait | |
| brain | faint | sail | taint | | |

eigh

sleigh

a

| acorn | fable | label | stable |

Unit 2 'ee'
ee

asleep	breeze	deep	redeem	sneeze	teem	
bee	cheep	see	seem	squeeze	weep	
bleep	creep	feel	sleep	steep	wheeze	

ea

beam	cheat	feast	ice-cream	preach	seal	wheat
beast	cream	flea	leap	reach	seam	yeast
beat	defeat	gleam	least	reap	seat	
bleach	each	heap	peach	retreat	steam	
cheap	eat	heat	pleat	scream	team	

e

| be | he | me | she | we | |

y

| baby | bunny | ferry | lady | sunny | |
| berry | cherry | funny | runny | very | |

Unit 3 'igh'
igh

igh	fight	knight	might	plight	slight	upright
bright	flight	light	night	right	tight	uptight
delight	fright	midnight	outright	sight	tonight	

Appendix 6 Word banks

i–e

advice	brine	dive	lice	nice	spike	twine
airline	combine	drive	like	recline	strike	valentine
alike	define	hike	live	pike	strive	vice
alive	dice	hive	mice	price	survive	whine
arrive	dislike	jive	mine	shine	trike	wine

y

| dry | shy | sly | spy | sty |

ie

| die | lie | pie | tie |

i

| behind | blind | remind | rind | wind |
| bind | grind | rewind | unkind | |

Unit 4 'ow'

ow

| arrow | own | show | thrown |
| flow | row | sow | |

o–e

alone	close	hose	prone	smoke	throne	woke
bone	cone	lone	propose	stole	tone	zone
console	dole	mole	provoke	stone	trombone	
chose	drone	ozone	role	suppose	xylophone	
clone	expose	pole	sole	those	vole	

oa

afloat	coal	float	gloat	oat	stoat
boast	coast	foal	loan	roast	throat
cloak	croak	goal	moat	soak	toast

o

| almost | ghost | host | post | utmost |

Unit 5 'oo'

oo

balloon	coop	harpoon	loop	scoop	stoop	troop
boot	drool	hoot	maroon	scoot	swoop	tycoon
brood	droop	lagoon	mood	shoot	tool	typhoon
cartoon	fool	loot	school	spoon	toot	whoop

u–e

acute	crude	dispute	flute	minute	pollute	salute
brute	cute	dune	gratitude	mute	prune	tune
chute	dilute	exclude	June	nude	rude	

ew

| chew | stew | drew | crew |

ue

| barbecue | cue | glue | pursue | sue |

Appendix 6 Word banks

Unit 6 'ou'

ou

announce	flounce	louse	pounce	scout	stout
bounce	foul	lout	pout	snout	throughout
clout	house	ounce	pronounce	spouse	trout

ow

allow	eyebrow	growl	pow	scowl	vow
bow	fowl	meow	prowl	sow	vowel
brow	how	owl	row	towel	wow

Unit 7 'ar'

ar

afar	ark	dart	hark	part	smart	tar
ajar	bark	depart	harm	remark	spar	tart
alarm	charm	embark	lark	scar	spark
apart	chart	guitar	mark	shark	start

a (southern accents only)

| only) | bask | cask | contrast | mask | past | vast |
| aghast | blast | cast | flask | mast | task |

Unit 8 'ur'

ir

| ladybird | stir | swirl | third | whirr |

ur

| absurd | burst | curse | purse | spur |
| blur | churn | occur | slur |

er

| her | herd | nerd | prefer |

Unit 9 'air'

air

| airy | fairy | hair | mid-air |
| dairy | flair | lair | unfair |

are

| dare | glare | mare | scare | software |
| ensnare | hare | prepare | share |

ear

| bear | tear | swear |

Unit 10 'or'

or

acorn	chord	forlorn	scorn	sworn	unicorn
adorn	corn	horn	shorn	thorn	worn
afford	ford	record	sword	torn

ore

| bore | core | forehead | gore | tore |

oor

| door | floor | indoor | outdoor |

aw

| claw | flaw | law | raw | straw | thaw |

Appendix 6 Word banks

Unit 11 'oy'
oy

loyal royal

oi

coil oil recoil soil spoil toil turmoil

Unit 12 'ear' 'ire'
ear

appear disappear near shear spear
clear gear rear smear tear

ire

bonfire dire enquire spire tire
desire empire inspire squire umpire

Get Spelling! Book 2

Below are further examples of words containing the graphemes focussed on in the *Get Spelling! Book 2* units.

Unit 1 soft c

place	palace	thrice	niece	truce	choice
plaice	malice	precise	cease	spruce	voice
replace	slice	imprecise	piece	force	rejoice
misplace	splice	parcel	masterpiece	source	decent
surface	spice	fleece	juice	enforce	recent

Unit 2 soft g
-ge

charge	outrage	damage	average	huge	binge	lunge
barge	voyage	storage	coverage	refuge	dinge	urge
cage	garbage	wastage	advantage	bulge	hinge	splurge
rage	package	language	spillage	indulge	cringe	merge
sage	shrinkage	vantage	manage	change	whinge	submerge
wage	bandage	advantage	encourage	range	lounge	
enrage	mileage	vicarage	courage	arrange	scrounge	

-dge

| slodge | dislodge/ | fudge | smudge | edge | porridge |
| stodge | budge | sludge | knowledge | sledge | |

There are no further words for Units 3 and 4.

Unit 5 -le
-le

circle	rabble	tumble	smuggle	rattle	castle	needle
candle	bubble	stumble	snuggle	bottle	muscle	
snuggle	stubble	baffle	struggle	pickle	article	
babble	warble	snaffle	trample	trickle	bicycle	
scrabble	nimble	raffle	simple	crumple	particle	
dabble	thimble	waffle	topple	crinkle	gargle	
gabble	humble	bubble	cattle	example	crumble	

Word banks

Unit 6 -al -il -el

-al

herbal	pedal	dial	actual	mural	removal
central	signal	loyal	mammal	central	interval
verbal	genial	gradual	oral	signal	
rascal	jovial	annual	choral	formal	

-il

stencil   devil

-el

rebel	shovel	trowel	jewel	travel	hazel
novel	caramel	vowel	fuel	snivel	
grovel	towel	cruel	parcel	drivel	

Unit 7 -en -on -an -in

-on

| ribbon | common | melon | prison |
| pardon | apron | fashion | pigeon |

-en

sudden   wooden   often   sharpen   deepen   even   oven

Unit 8 -tion -sion

-tion

nation	illustration	congregation	desperation	ambition	election	eruption
station	conversation	examination	generation	tradition	diction	
foundation	dedication	donation	cooperation	promotion	friction	
formation	medication	decoration	celebration	pollution	attention	
indignation	qualification	moderation	registration	solution	caption	
occupation	classification	exploration	sensation	action	perception	
formation	location	preparation	condensation	fraction	option	

-sion

precision   illusion   collusion   inclusion   intrusion   confusion   transfusion

Unit 9 -ent -ant -ment

-ent

| obedient | fluent | resident | transparent | decent |
| client | president | talent | current | recent |

-ant

defiant   truant   redundant   arrogant   participant   currant

-ment

management	arrangement	commitment	excitement	document
document	embarrassment	disappointment	advertisement	patient
attachment	punishment	pavement	amusement	

Unit 10 -ence -ance

-ence

sentence   intelligence   audience   experience   science   reference   essence

-ance

| annoyance | ambulance | defiance | balance | nuisance |
| entrance | brilliance | arrogance | assistance | |

Word banks

Unit 11 -ous -cious -tious

-ous

joyous	arduous	sumptuous	courteous	courageous	odious
continuous	strenuous	marvellous	hideous	anxious	

-cious

vicious   malicious

Unit 12 schwa -ure

-ure

moisture	lecture	adventure	texture	sure	enclosure
sculpture	architecture	posture	mixture	displeasure	
departure	puncture	gesture	injure	closure	

Unit 13 -ible -ibly -able

-able

agreeable	breakable	thinkable	reasonable	considerable
enjoyable	drinkable	approachable	bearable	removable

-ible

edible	credible	audible	visible	sensible

Unit 14 -ful -fully

playful / playfully	useful / usefully	skilful / skilfully	forgetful
scornful / scornfully	awfu l/ awfully	respectful / respectfully	

There are no Word banks for Get Spelling! Book 3 as the Units focus on spelling specific words.

Read Write Inc. Spelling and the Primary Framework for Literacy

Read Write Inc. Spelling covers all of the Word structure and spelling requirements of the Primary Framework for Literacy as detailed below. When children are below National Curriculum Level 2a (English Language 5–14 Level B) *Read Write Inc. Phonics* can be used to teach the earlier stages of spelling.

Core learning in literacy by strand

6. Word structure and spelling

Year 2
- *Spell with increasing accuracy and confidence, drawing on word recognition and knowledge of word structure, and spelling patterns including common inflections and use of double letters*
  Get Spelling! Book 1 focuses on spelling patterns and how words are structured to ensure children's confidence and accuracy is developed. There is a section devoted to inflections.
- *Read and spell less common alternative graphemes including trigraphs*
  A range of alternative graphemes including trigraphs are taught in *Get Spelling! Books 1 and 2*.

Year 3
- *Spell high and medium frequency words*
  Get Spelling! Books 1, 2 and 3 all cover spelling of high and medium frequency words.
- *Recognise a range of prefixes and suffixes, understanding how they modify meaning and spelling, and how they assist in decoding long complex words*
  Get Spelling! Books 1, 2 and 3 all show how adding suffixes affect the meaning of words. Children are taught how words with prefixes and suffixes can be 'unpicked' to the root word to aid their understanding of long and complex words.
- *Spell unfamiliar words using known conventions including grapheme-phoneme correspondences and morphological rules*
  Children are taught to spell by using grapheme-phoneme correspondences and understanding the morphology of words throughout the programme.

Year 4
- *Use knowledge of phonics, morphology and etymology to spell new and unfamiliar words*
  Children are taught to spell by focussing on the phonics and morphology of words throughout the programme. *Get Spelling! Book 3* focuses on the etymology of words.
- *Distinguish the spelling and meaning of common homophones*
  Homophones are focussed on in *Get Spelling! Books 1 and 2*.
- *Know and apply common spelling rules*
  Common spelling rules are taught throughout and children are reminded of them via 'Spelling tips'.
- *Develop a range of personal strategies for learning new and irregular words*
  Strategies for learning irregular words are taught and practised throughout *Get Spelling! Books 1, 2 and 3* and consolidated in the *Spelling Log Book* practice.

Year 5
- *Spell words containing unstressed vowels*
  Children are taught to spell words containing unstressed vowels in *Get Spelling! Books 2 and 3*, breaking up words for spelling using 'full value syllables', e.g. for 'medal', 'distant', 'behaviour'.
- *Know and use less common prefixes and suffixes such as im-, ir-, -cian*
  A range of less common prefixes and suffixes are taught in *Get Spelling! Book 3*.
- *Group and classify words according to their spelling patterns and meanings*
  Children are taught this throughout the programme.

Year 6
- *Spell familiar words correctly and employ a range of strategies to spell difficult and unfamiliar words*
  Strategies for learning difficult and unfamiliar words are taught and practised throughout *Get Spelling! Books 1, 2 and 3* and consolidated in the *Spelling Log Book* practice.
- *Use a range of appropriate strategies to edit, proofread and correct spelling in their own work, on paper and on screen*
  Children are taught this throughout the programme through a variety of activities.